> Dean Fraser is grateful that he gets to [do what he loves] most, which is create beautiful things [for] others and for his legacy to stand the [test of time. To be as] relevant and appreciated in a hundred years, as he is dedicated for his creativity to be today.

Dean Fraser shows how evolving comes from living, making mistakes which are not really mistakes but learning, walking our talk and sometimes tripping up a few times before we finally get the message about what we need in order to grow - NEW DAWN MAGAZINE

Dean Fraser sees his mission in life to spread some much-needed laughter and love in this world - INDIE SHAMAN MAGAZINE

Can a book really be considered healing? A Healing For Gaia had a lot to live up to with the title! These poetic narratives more than do...be they inspirational, thought provoking or just downright entertainingly off-the-wall! Absorb yourself within these pages and leave the cares of the world behind for a little while - PSYCHIC NEWS MAGAZINE

About The Poet

Born a month before the Spring Equinox some years ago Dean Fraser feels a connection to all of nature beauteous and green.

He is a poet, holistic storyteller and dowsing teacher.

He enjoys being out amongst nature rather than in cities.

So much for the biography. Dean prefers his energy and actions to speak for themselves.

A Healing For Gaia

A Celebration Of Life and Living

Dean Fraser

2020 for Alive to Thrive Ltd

Copyright © Dean Fraser 2020

Dean Fraser has asserted his right under the Copyright, Designs and Patents Act 1988 to be identified as the author of this book and work.

All rights reserved. No part of this publication may be reproduced, stored in a retrieval system or transmitted in any form or by any means, electronic, photocopying, recording or otherwise, without the prior permission of the copyright owner.

ISBN 978-1719209489

Although the author and publisher have made every effort to ensure that the information in this book was correct at press time, the author and publisher do not assume and hereby disclaim any liability to any party for any loss, damage, or disruption caused by errors or omissions, whether such errors or omissions result from negligence, accident, or any other cause. This book is not intended as a substitute for the medical advice of medical professionals. The reader should regularly consult a chosen medical professional in matters relating to his/her health and particularly with respect to any symptoms that may require diagnosis or medical attention.

Contents

    Page no

About The Poet	02
Introduction	09

PART ONE – LIFE

1967	12
Words Of Power	15
Understanding Begins With Ourselves	17
Earth Spirit	18
A Gift To You	21
A Healing For Gaia	22
Oneness	23
To The Mountain To Freedom	24
Rising Above It All	26
Eyes Open Wide	27
Oranges To Teach Us All	28
Dreams	29
Endless Possibilities	31
Trust In You	32
Inspiration In A Rose	33

City Life – Follow Your Bliss	34
The Seasons	36
Becoming	38
Journey's End	40
Summer Rain	41
To Dream Of Greatness	42
Quantum Stairway	43
Questioning	44
Wisdom Of The Tree	47
Living Within Love	48
Mirrored Imagination	49
Footsteps	50

PART TWO– LIVING

All The Things	56
Ancestors	58
Dragonfly	59
Quiet	60
Labels	61
The Serene Moon	63
21st Century Vegan	65
Inspired By Zen	67
So Many Changes	68
The Boots	70
Realisation	71

Reverse The Polarity	72
What About Me?	73
Connections	74
Looking For Signs	75
The Wisdom Of Children	76
Reasons For Getting Up	77
Be A Helicopter Pilot	78
Time For Action	79
Global Island	80
The Non-Spiritual, Spiritual Poem	81
Perfectly Imperfect	83
Meet The Dream Stealers	85
Magic Gems	86
Beauty Of Your Nature	88
Who Is Creating You?	89
Dragons	92
The Loving Ending	94

For the complete harmonic experience of these poems
A Healing For Gaia is also available as an MP3 audiobook music download.

Introduction

This is a concept poetry book.

It all started with me wishing to explore the meaning of life and why we are here on this beautiful planet at this time. To achieve this I took as a starting point inspiration from music. The intention became producing a book embodying some of the spirit of those paradigm shifting ambient concept albums created by the more esoterically inclined artists and bands over the decades.

Looking through the poetry and lyrics which came through me from my higher-self as I wrote this, I can only feel deeply grateful it does fulfil what I lovingly set out to realise and dare I say a little more.

Enjoy the experience of A Healing For Gaia! May it inspire all of you who really feel this book to find higher love within yourselves; to cherish the precious gift of this incarnation and revere the amazing home we all share - our Earth.

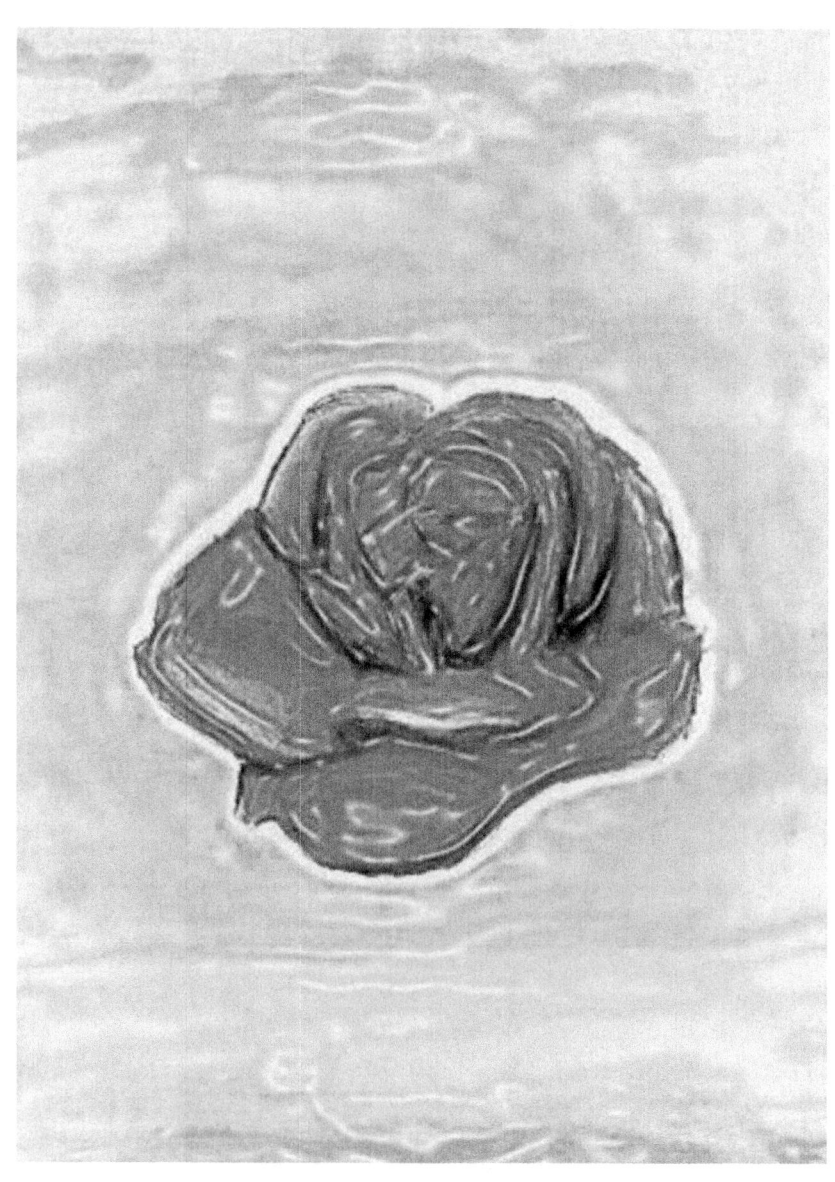

In A Sense After Salvador – Dean Fraser

Part One – Life

1967

She loved the Summer of Love.

Transcendental meditation.

Yoga.

Psychedelic art.

Dylan and Donovan travelled with her through life.

She discovered her real self in that latter part of the 60's.

Optimistic for the future.

She had a child now.

Born into his incarnation as the Summer of Love began.

Raising him according to her intuition.

The next decade would see changes.

In fashion.

Attitudes.

Brown and orange side by side in home décor.

Chopper bikes.

Double denim.

The anger of punk rock.

Here in 1967 she is open minded.

She feels the love.

A hippie at heart.

Like so many who experienced the Summer Of Love.

Through this mystery called life.

Her son learns about himself.

Later he would also meditate.

Seek the meaning of his existence.

The bodies we wear may change.

Through the decades on this bluey-green planet.

Some things remain constant.

Our still point.

Our authentic self.

Once discovered, never to be undiscovered.

She was a hippie at heart.

And would remain so for all her life.

What a legacy to leave…

peace

out

WORDS OF POWER

Words.

Words.

Words.

So many words.

So many words.

So many words.

Words of threat.

Words of bullying.

Words of thoughtlessness.

Words can crush any potential.

Enough!

Words.

Words.

Words.

So many words.

So many words.

So many words.

Words of encouragement.

Words of support.

Words to lend a Loving hand.

Words can move any mountain.

UNDERSTANDING BEGINS WITH OURSELVES

So many feel the need to fight,
living life with no inner light.
Why do so many appal,
simple fact that Love is all.
My desire all lost souls see,
potential for all they can be.
Life make of what we will,
finding our own truths until,
our future to be shaping, moulding,
parallel with our learning unfolding.
Emotional balance only natural.
Energy, happiness becomes factual.
Never was anyone else to blame.
Personal responsibility now reclaim.
Within us all expanding,
ourselves to be understanding.

EARTH SPIRIT

Taking my inspiration from the green green wood,
home to Herne the Hunter and good Robin Hood.
Sunlight sparkling through the canopy of trees,
botanical ecosystem living in harmony with ease.
A symphony of nature provided by birds singing,
natural is perfect, meditative energy I am bringing.

Taking my inspiration from the mountain top,
rising high into the sky like it will never stop.
The sunset transcending anything seen before,
reflected in the mirrored lake on the valley floor.
Strongest winds attempting to dislodge me to a fall,
high upon the mountain, meditating, taking in it all.

Taking my inspiration from the magical seashore,
meditation upon the beach as the tide comes ashore.
Secluded bay far from people, for once truly alone,
seagulls diving in and out of the white foam.
Sun transforms water as a million diamonds,
mesmerizing waves roaring in their guidance.

Remembering these wondrous places within my mind,

loving gratitude meditative inner peace combined.

Feeling magical appreciation for freely given beauty,

simply standing gazing in awe at all of nature's bounty.

Look outward and look within as Earth gives freely,

Thank you, thank you, thank you most deeply.

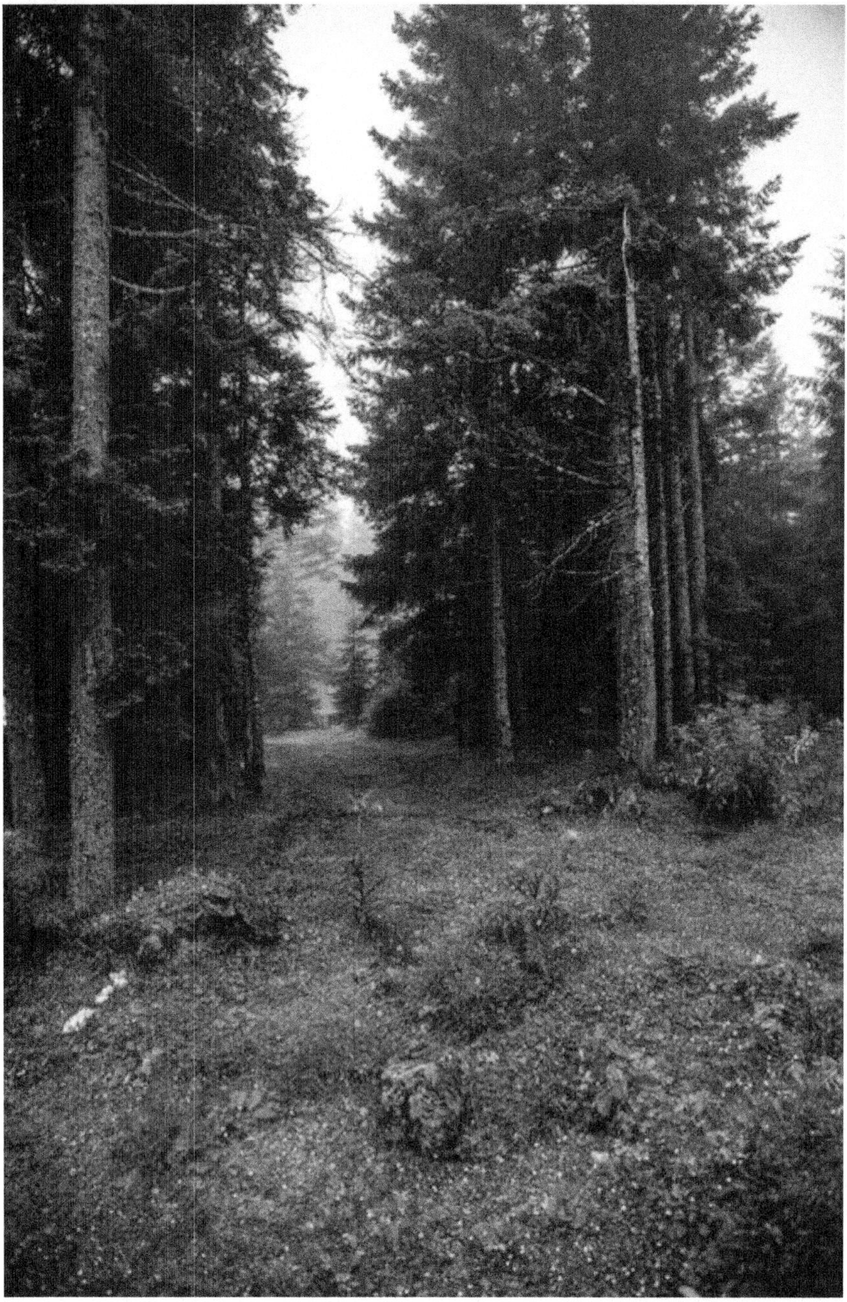

A GIFT TO YOU

Some people say that they cannot use the power of their mind,
they say it is impossible to vision anything.
Nothing to inspire them, nothing deep inside for them to seek,
nothing to make their heart and soul sing.
Think of a beautiful tropical island looking like paradise on Earth,
palm trees gently swaying in the sea breeze.
The healing warmth of the sun as it kisses lightly upon your skin,
relaxing, for once enjoying being at total ease.
Walking barefoot making virgin footprints in the hot sand,
feeling it coming up between your toes.
Beautiful birdsong fills the air as the waves wash gently,
inhaling the purest air in through your nose.

A HEALING FOR GAIA

Forgotten Stone Circle a new day is dawning.

Transcendent sunrise welcomes in the morning.

Sunshine warming us, the dew laden ground.

At one with nature as we chant sacred sound.

Resonating with landscape, the stones, the past.

Feeling our ancestor's wisdom here amassed.

Help us open the eyes of those unable to yet see.

Protect our home Gaia in her transcendent glory.

Denizens of the stones you revered this sacred land.

Let us together take the unenlightened by the hand.

Respect one another, Love projected in all actions.

Harmony in every thought, peace within reactions.

ONENESS

Please help open my mind,

rationality limits potential.

Quieten pointless ponderings.

Let my mind be free.

A thousand random thoughts vie for attention.

Only the chatter of mundaneness.

Never did mean anything.

Time for a new paradigm.

Overdue awakening within.

Intuition, then inner knowing.

To be still from inside out.

To listen to nothing.

Calmness permeates.

At last…

TO THE MOUNTAIN TO FREEDOM

She had journeyed far from the valley below.
Through many trials compelled to undergo.
Ascent the hardest choice and yet no choice.
Listening as she had to her own inner voice.

Her focus, her life spent climbing upwards.
Often two steps forward, one backwards.
Determinedly she continued her endless quest.

Grateful to know the mountain, deeply blessed.

Looking back she sees obstacles now long gone.
She knew they would pass if she only pushed on.
Trials and tribulations tested if she is faint hearted.
Immeasurable distance from where she started.

Her ascent to the summit, her own path taken.
One dimensional existence long since forsaken.
And yet the path now also seems to be gone.
She pondered with an open mind thereupon.

Panic and worry having long since been banished.
Looking back every obstacle has now also vanished.
Considering her journey in her own minds eye,
dawning realisation hit her, now she could FLY!

RISING ABOVE IT ALL

Polarities bring decisions to make.
Is that still point true or just fake?
Acts of others testing our poise.
So full of anger, making some noise.
Ahhh, turn away or get involved?
Responses needing to be resolved.

To waste our energy with pointless futility?
Get angry as well, speak words of hostility?
Better now focus on our own pathway.
Personal journey so well underway.
Why need we lower our reactions,
for the sake of such un-evolved actions?

Those seeking to grow will always encounter,
people wanting to bring us onto their downer.
Needing a way of keeping our calm.
Living within love, causing no harm.
Why not just smile and cheerfully say?
"I send you love and have a good day!"

EYES OPEN WIDE

With purest open heart.

Negativity now depart.

In beauty walking.

Inner voice talking.

Cleansed, whole.

Mind, body, soul.

Harmonious living.

Smiles easily giving.

Complete inside.

All eyes open wide.

Still point that is sought.

All actions all thought.

Transformation undergo.

To understand, to know.

Truly deeply fathom.

Love in every atom.

ORANGES TO TEACH US ALL

The meaning of orange,

the colour of no rage.

Hidden inside orange,

lays waiting no rage.

Oh mysterious orange,

being free from rage.

Wear the shirt orange,

living a life of no rage.

Ever enough orange?

Being free from rage.

Orangey is the orange,

no rage is all the rage.

Hail the happy orange,

the essence of no rage.

DREAMS

The plumber dreamt of being a musician.
The musician dreamt of being a magician.
The magician dreamt of being a florist.
The florist dreamt of being a chemist.
The chemist dreamt of being a judge.
The judge dreamt of making fudge.

Got to make all those dreams come true.
Take action, do it now, it's down to you.

The mechanic dreamt of being a meteorologist.
The meteorologist dreamt of being a sociologist.
The sociologist dreamt of being a train driver.
The train driver dreamt of being a deep-sea diver.
The deep-sea diver dreamt of being a psychiatrist.
The psychiatrist dreamt of being a unicyclist.

Got to make all those dreams come true.
Take action, do it now, it's down to you.

The grandmother dreamt of being at University.

The student dreamt of being at sea.

The sailor dreamt of being at home.

The sailor's wife felt oh so alone.

The loner made a wish to the power's above.

Please let me find my only one true love.

Got to make all those dreams come true.

Take action, do it now, it's down to you.

ENDLESS POSSIBILITIES

Confidence comes from self-knowing.

Knowing is to journey within.

Within is the source of all wisdom.

Wisdom is to truly master life.

Life is about self-knowing.

Knowing oneself is growing.

Growing is the true path.

Paths all lead to inner wisdom.

Wisdom is an acceptance.

Acceptance is to know oneself.

Oneself the true source of knowing.

Knowing, yet never knowing all.

All we exist for is growing.

Growing onwards mastering life.

Life, needing to manifest wisdom.

Wisdom knowing eternally growing.

Endless possibilities…

TRUST IN YOU

What is false and what is real?

Can we really trust the way we feel?

Are perceptions the ultimate illusions?

Do minds create the greatest delusions?

Books partially helping in growing,

better attuned to our inner knowing.

Re-learning all knowledge once we knew.

The energy of pure love to eternally renew.

Anti-war requires a war to exist.

Pro-peace and war will desist…

INSPIRATION IN A ROSE

Living the urban life and wondering how,

is inner connection possible here and now?

Inspiration in the city always for those who see,

it is in every person, flower and tree.

Walking these busy streets looking around,

it is alive in the buildings, the sound.

Yet here is nature, she never quite goes,

find yourself a park and go smell a rose.

CITY LIFE – FOLLOW YOUR BLISS

His friends thought what a pity,
abandoning his job in the city.
They judged him to be quite mad,
early mid-life crisis, how sad.

Next, he distributed some of his wealth,
considered it essential for good health.
Trinkets of a life he had turned away from,
and pretty soon he will also be long gone.

A Scottish island to be his new home,
clean air, wildness, freedom to roam.
He will craft arty things from driftwood,
his life harmonized natural and good.

His inner voice he could no longer ignore,
happiness his reality like never before.
A simpler new life and his soul is at ease.
to inner bliss and contentment, he has the keys.

Sometimes he ponders all the wasted years,

all the deals he did; blood, sweat and tears.

"Life carries on there, they won't think of me,

my decision to seek big skies and blue sea".

From his window every season looks pretty,

winters are harsh, but then so is the city.

If they are happy in the city, he is glad they are,

for himself he is grateful he has come so far…

THE SEASONS

The whole forest awakens into Spring.

Buds and leaves freshly formed on trees.

Bluebells carpet the ground.

Soon, very soon all life reborn,

in anticipation of Summer.

Summer sun a forest resplendent.

Harmonic balance of existence.

Birds share their songs generously.

Warmth filters through canopies of branches.

and it seems so long 'til Autumn.

Autumn brings a gentle winding down.

Scenery thrills in red, gold and green.

A thousand scents vie for attention.

Squirrels preparing as a warning,

soon it will be upon us, Winter.

Winter and a forest turned white with frost.

Mist drifts eerily between the trees.

Thinking back through time it seems so close.

Those fresh Spring days, halcyon Summer sun,

the preparing for sleep time of Autumn.

We start out in our Spring, our leaves unfurling.

Maturity comes and we reach our Summer.

Cease growing and our Autumn arrives,

Winter brings an opportunity to re-think, change,

seek the path of growth – experience eternal Spring!

BECOMING

I am the life-giving sun.

I am the fertile land.

I am the fresh rain.

I am the wild wind.

I am the white snow.

I am the rivers and sea.

I am the living forest.

I am the proud stag.

I am the humble ant.

I am the distant past.

I am the unknown future.

I am the gentle whale.

I am the predatory lion.

I am the wisdom of ages.

I am the innocent baby.

I am the black night sky.

I am the sparkling stars.

I am the welcome sunrise.

I am the power to renew.

I am divine.

And so are you…

> Seek YOUR Truth and Set Yourself FREE!

JOURNEY'S END

Look within for answers.

Always the only way.

Seek YOUR truth and set YOURSELF free.

Introspection long overdue.

Inner mirrored.

Seek YOUR truth and set YOURSELF free.

Finally coming home.

The you of you.

Seek YOUR truth and set YOURSELF free.

SUMMER RAIN

To walk in the cleansing summer rain,

nirvana for humans and parched ground.

Pine trees, roses, the damp earth

and a thousand other scents.

All at once brought alive,

teasing our senses with their beauty,

Thoroughly soaking wet and caring not,

simple joys of being alive…

TO DREAM OF GREATNESS

I like seaside piers; in a parallel world I'm a Victorian engineer.

In this world I am mostly polite and mostly sincere.

I like architecture: in a parallel world I designed Carnegie Hall.

In this world I just sketch buildings, taking in it all.

I like trains; in a parallel world I drive them to Kathmandu.

In this world no leaves or snow on the track will do.

I like trees; in a parallel world I saved the Amazon Rainforest.

In this world against a tree I simply like to sit and rest.

I like walking; in a parallel world whole continents I slowly cross.

In this world after a days hike exhausted I come across.

I like dreaming; in a parallel world I follow dreams and never fate.

In this world make them happen as well…why wait?

QUANTUM STAIRWAY

Stood on the middle step of the stairs.

Ascend or descend?

Eternal decision to make…

QUESTIONING

It took me a while,

yet there is not a clock ticking here.

Looking outwards I observed life.

Pondering inwardly.

When the student is ready.

I know the answer now,

oh finally, the truth is revealed!

The great unanswered mystery.

A "How to" manual to life.

Well, it is all about questions.

Every time we think,

we ask ourselves questions.

Even opting out of making decisions,

first requires we ask of ourselves…

Questions.

How to make this work?

To transcend the treadmill existence?

The answer became crystal clear.

Still ask ourselves questions

and make them amazing ones!

Stretch our comfort zones.

Live in the zone.

Raising our own standards.

Our expectations of what is possible.

Yes, questions.

Amazing questions…

More amazing answers.

Creates an amazing life.

Dare to dare ourselves!

The quality of questions is everything.

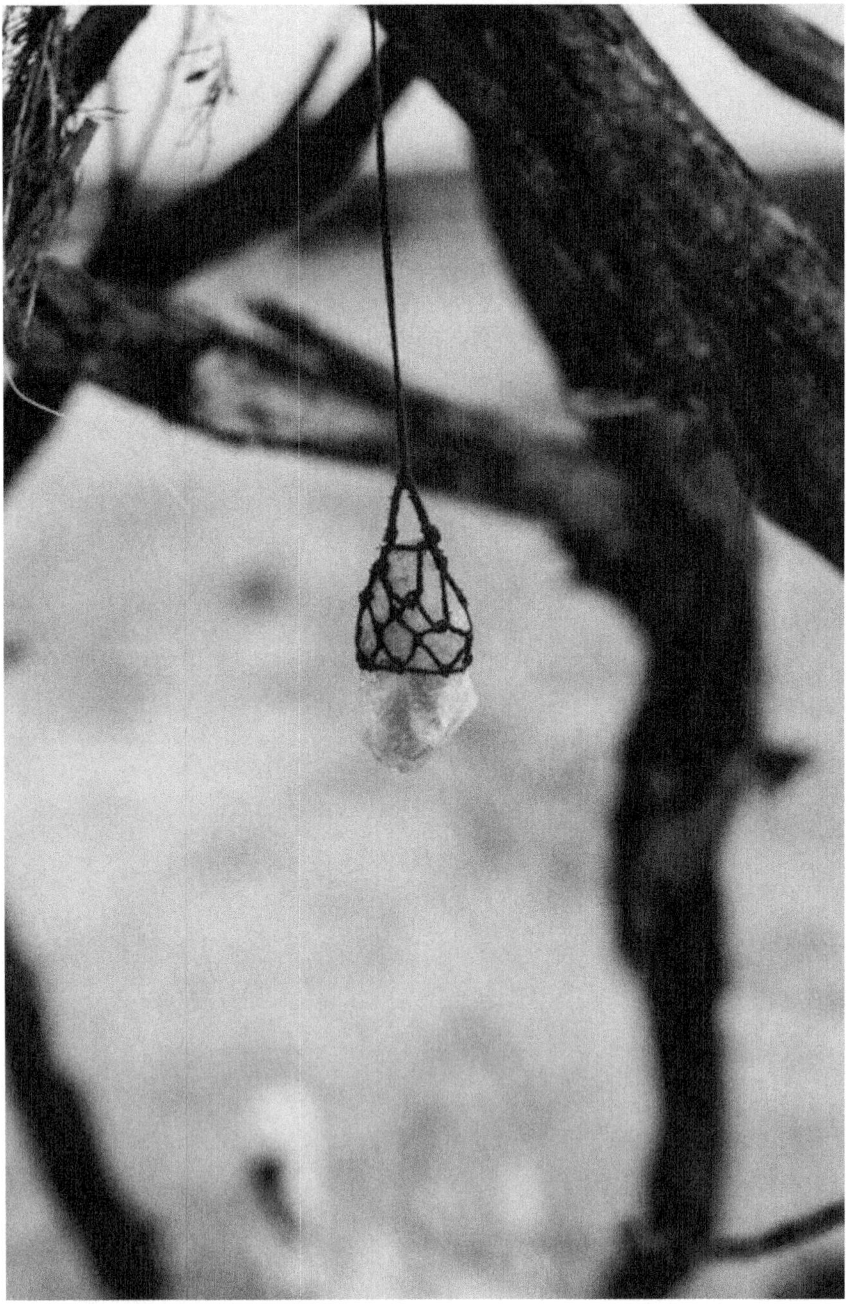

WISDOM OF THE TREE

He has lived longer than you or I,

standing tall amongst his forest of friends.

What makes this tree so special?

Why are so many compelled to visit this exact tree?

Leave offerings in his branches,

bury gifts between his roots…

Wisdom Tree gives freely of his counsel.

Wisdom Tree communicates clearly.

For those with ears open enough to hear.

Humanity drawn to ask favours from Wisdom Tree.

Questions.

Always more questions.

Some mysteries defy logic.

All is as it needs to be then.

LIVING WITHIN LOVE

Intuiting multi-dimensional truths.

The art of being.

Harmonious communication with every atom spiralling.

The highest vibrational energy.

Illuminated pathway.

Intuition followed.

Emotions guiding.

Existing beyond dimensions.

Being love.

Living love.

Limitless within love.

MIRRORED IMAGINATION

Look into the windows of my soul.

As I study the windows of your soul.

All at once reflected to me.

Portal to your higher self.

Oneness.

FOOTSTEPS

Back in the mists of time we walked these shores.

This view we have seen.

Meditated on this rock.

To the sound of waves lapping gently.

Footsteps, walking in our own past.

Back in the mists of time we walked in this forest.

These trees our friends.

Meditated leant against the old oak.

To the sound of the birdsong chorus.

Footsteps, walking in our own past.

Back in the mists of time we climbed this mountain.

Winter's snow and spring's wildflowers.

Meditated in the heart of the cave.

To the sound of the eagle's distant calls.

Footsteps, walking in our own past.

Back in the mists of time we lived by the seasons.

In harmony with all that is natural.

Meditated under the bluest sky.

To the sound of the earth's heartbeat.

Footsteps, walking in our own past.

Back in the mists of time I looked into your eyes.

Hearts and souls eternally connected.

Meditated beside one another.

To the sound of eternity.

Footsteps, walking in our own past.

Footsteps – Dean Fraser

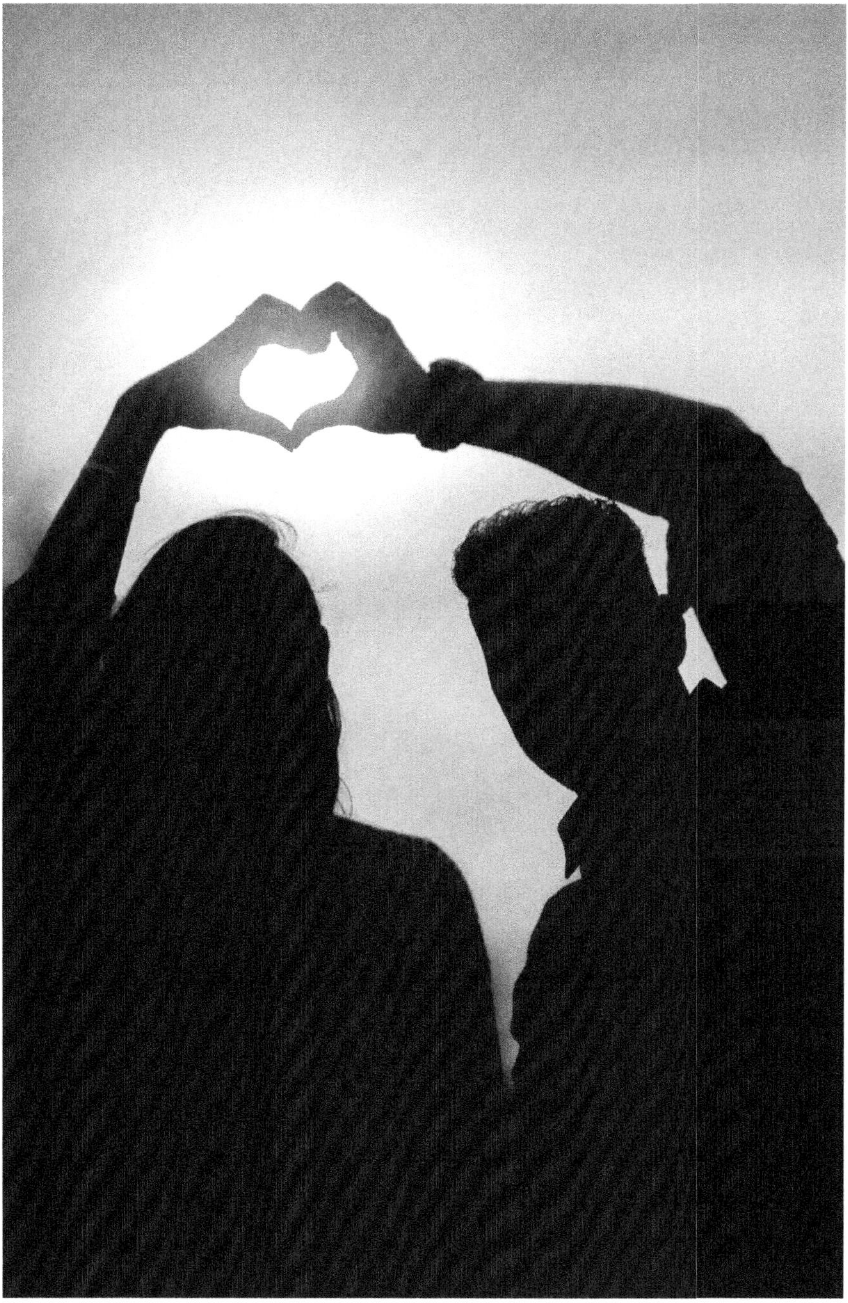

Part Two – Living

RETURNING TO DREAMS

And so once more we return to dreams.

That eternal truth as it always seems.

Got to make all those dreams come true.

Take action, do it now, it's down to you.

It being absolutely essential.

Living life to our potential.

Doing nothing standing by.

Authentic self, truth to deny.

This path being soul treason.

Always an excuse, a reason.

Turning away from where we need to be.

Closing minds to our eternal liberty.

My reality took a while to sink in.

Inner voice screaming, making a din.

To be creative my path to take.

Safe, boring life I had to forsake.

Thoughts…words…emotion,

messages of love, deep devotion,

my role in life was to spread.

Heart naturally ruling my head.

Got to make all those dreams come true.

Take action, do it now, it's down to you.

ANCESTORS

Are we happier than our ancestors were?
Are we more stressed if we dare to compare?
Simpler lives close to nature they did lead.
These days all the pressure to materially succeed.
Alien to our ancestors, their life by the seasons.
If we unhappy time to look within for the reasons.

Our connection to Gaia replaced by online life.
News channels sharing stories of war and strife.
Reclaim our birth-right, our DNA from the past.
Waits right these inside us, all wisdom amassed.
Unlock for ourselves, discover first-hand.
Journey within to reconnect to the land.

Let's be happier like our ancestors were.
Less stress now when we care to compare.

DRAGONFLY

Most beautiful dragonfly you ever did see.

Descends to land upon my left knee.

We looked one another deep in the eye.

Then with a wink, it flew away into the sky.

QUIET

So many people busy talking at us.

Aggressively vocalising what they discuss.

Try with great passion to change our mind.

Often using insults or expressions unkind.

Loudly to make us see their point of view.

Failing to listen, through their hullabaloo.

Shhh…Listen to the silence…

LABELS

Which style of clothes we choose to wear.
Are those the right labels on show there?
Or supermarket jeans with matching top.
Did that bag come from an online shop?
Got to dress-up that look, make it "you".
Designer a must, branded training shoe.

Only one way to be powerfully able,
free ourselves from any kind of label.

We used to buy a car for what it did.
A choice that brand awareness soon undid.
If it does not wear the proper badge, it's tragic.
Of course, it is nice to have nice things, magic.
Buying into designer experience is only a sham.
For sure an Emperor's New Clothes kind of scam.

Only one way to be totally able,
free ourselves from any kind of label.

What is your job, who is your circle?

How to exist in this world so commercial?

How is your accent? Are you eloquent enough?

Are you geeky or perhaps considered hot stuff?

Wearing shades in winter only for the look.

Posting to impress to excess on Facebook.

Only one way to be totally able,

free ourselves from any kind of label.

Look within for the answers to the meaning of life.

Forget chasing labels, the cause of so much strife.

Look within, the answer has always been inside.

Let our own intuition still be our eternal guide.

Happiness our birth right and to be free of,

chasing those labels, and just feeling the love.

THE SERENE MOON

The Moon looked down upon the dwellers in the city.

Illuminated silent observer casting light.

People going about their life with such intense intent.

What lesson do you teach oh beautiful, serene moon?

Your light existing only as a reflection from the sun.

With your dark side so well hidden.

Just as we walk this earth.

Illuminated by a higher force.

Duality constantly at play.

Look upwards in the clear night.

Reminder to all to shine.

Reflecting brightly our beautiful serene us of us…

21ST CENTURY VEGAN

Choices we make as we face each day.

Which clothes to wear, cash or card to pay.

What to eat, what to drink, where to travel.

Look around reality and see it all unravel.

One choice I made, to embrace veganism.

Now dining out can cause a big schism.

Animal products I avoid in entirety.

Kind of out of step with the rest of society.

"But what do you eat?" I so often hear.

Let me tell you one more time, make it quite clear.

Nothing that could cause needless harm.

That come from rivers or lives on a farm.

Avoiding any animal ingredient,

I consider most expedient.

This story is all about me,

my choice to live cruelty free.

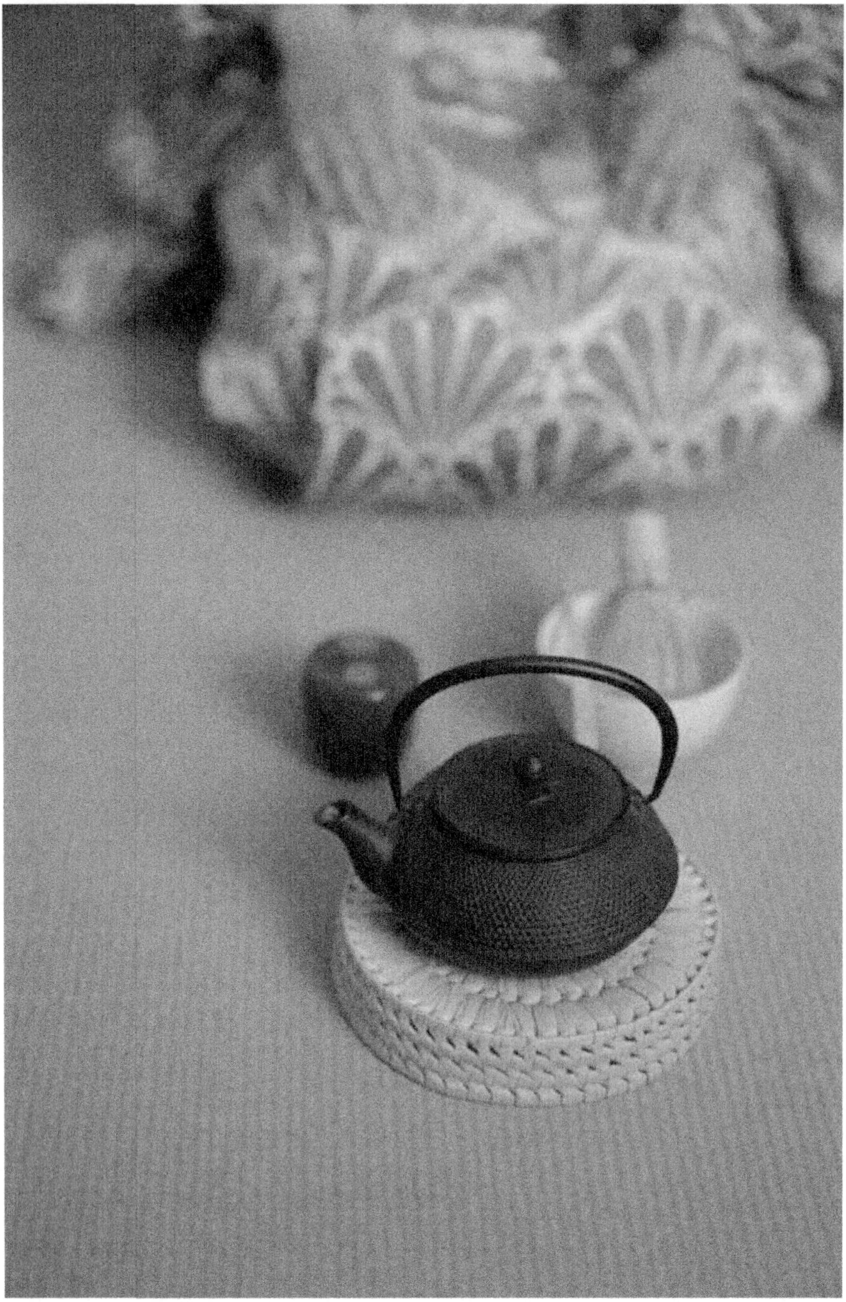

INSPIRED BY ZEN

In order to make good tea,

first you need the water.

Then add the tea

and leave to brew.

The combination greater

than the sum of its parts.

Without the tea,

all you end up,

is unfulfilled.

In order to evolve, grow,

first you need the desire.

Then add the will

and leave to brew.

The combination greater

than the sum of its parts.

Without the will,

all you end up,

is unfulfilled.

SO MANY CHANGES

Born into this World of mystery.

Exploring into greater understanding.

Schooling according to someone else's plan.

Nature teaching infinitely more.

Night sky fascinates.

Stars and moon familiar friends.

Healing others in innocence.

Rediscovering who I am.

Telling others of my dreams.

Falling mainly upon closed ears.

Yet keeping the dreams all the same.

Forth into adulthood.

Career paths to take.

The dreams remain.

Maturity of responsibility.

Others depend upon my labours.

Co-workers looking upon me as vital.

Still I seek more.

I love words and healing.

My dreams entice me.

Always the dreams.

Dreams there to be followed.

The past to be forgiven.

In deepest gratitude for the journey.

Oh to heal with words.

Inspire, just as words inspire.

More changes, yet I am constant.

THE BOOTS

Walking boots are donned early morn.

Into nature witness the rising dawn.

Spring Solstice, what could inspire more?

Forgotten stone circle upon empty moor.

Coolness felt upon my essentially bare feet.

Eyes closed, sense sunrise, harmony complete.

Warming rays invigorating body and soul.

Oneness with all elements, at once whole.

REALISATION

Sometimes introspection.

Sometimes isolation.

Ultimate revelation.

Ultimate elation.

Transcendent inspiration.

Transcendent realisation.

A higher purpose for existing.

Forever seeking, persisting.

Look within and look without end.

Make yourself your own best friend.

REVERSE THE POLARITY

In these strange times,

always looking for the signs.

Guidance as we go on our way,

paying heed without delay.

Signals from the Universe,

thoughts polarity to reverse.

Negativity will depart.

when we open our heart.

WHAT ABOUT ME?

I see them.

Seeking a bluer sky.

Those streets seemingly paved with gold.

A charmed life looked at from a distance.

What about me?

I am grateful to waken this morning.

Another day of possibilities.

I make my reality.

CONNECTIONS

Our bodies borrowed from the universe.

Made of stardust.

Everywhere and nowhere at once.

Souls having a human experience.

Moving ego aside to freedom.

Inspiration guiding our actions.

Through universal connections.

How often the truth hides.

Right there in plain sight.

LOOKING FOR SIGNS

Sometimes life gives us a big flashing neon sign,

"Step this way please, your future is here, now is the time!"

Needing to be ready to act, seems illogical, feeling wary.

Take that action, embracing change, no matter how scary.

Finally, to be on the way to living our life how it should be.

When the chances come along, embracing our destiny.

THE WISDOM OF CHILDREN

Children have acting "as if" down to a fine art.

Role playing directly from their soul and heart.

Thinking back to childhood when we so easily role played.

Make believed we could be anything at all, unafraid.

"I'm a footballer" or "we're all cops now", as one we proclaim.

Oddly enough, I have found adult life is exactly the same…

REASONS FOR GETTING UP

Success quite simply getting out of bed as the day is dawning.

Giving thanks to be alive and looking forward to the morning.

Thinking "how will I make a difference in the world today?"

Smiling, feeling every experience gained on our pathway.

Living kindness embracing everyone as a matter of routine.

Then bed at night once more, happy with what we did in-between…

BE A HELICOPTER PILOT

A helicopter takes off vertically, just as we do when we say YES.
As new opportunities take us up to a new level of success.

A helicopter changes direction instantly flying across the sky.
As we can choose to listen to intuition, in the blinking of an eye,

A helicopter hovers, to land anywhere which seems interesting.
As we can see the bigger picture, overcoming anything limiting.

TIME FOR ACTION

Putting ourselves down, surest way to disempower.

A new style of thinking, all about energy and power.

Failing is a myth every time, here is our golden opportunity.

Next time lesson learned, now we have evolved an immunity.

Follow your bliss, so many truths being told in cliché.

Take those first steps right now, inaction is so yesterday.

GLOBAL ISLAND

Sark, idyllic island without a single car.
Anywhere you would wish to go, is not so far.
A relaxing life, taken at a much slower pace.
Everyone friendly, it is just that kind of place.
Always having time for a chilled conversation.
Local's attitude to life, like one long vacation.
Sure they work, often hard, yet never a chore.
They see it as adding to the community they adore.

Seems about perfect to me, wonder if you agree?
So perfect in fact, I would like to make a heartfelt plea.
Sark in the Channel Islands, microcosmic role model.
Scale up their template across the Earth to remodel.
New focuses, new priorities, new ways of being.
From the treadmill existence everyone be freeing.
Life about happiness, living love, global community.
Every nation as one, existing in perfect unity…

THE NON-SPIRITUAL, SPIRITUAL POEM

Fragrant tea rose.

Butterfly on the nose.

Warmth of the sun.

Cinnamon sticky bun.

Sole fell off my shoe.

Stick it back on with glue.

Sunflower bumble bee.

Ferryman pay the fee.

Fragrances sweet pea.

Externalized inner chi.

Question all we see.

Rejecting or agree.

Find our way home.

Imprinted genome.

All yew trees know.

The way to grow.

Immortality there within.

Our spiritual arboreal twin.

Locked deep in our DNA.

We will understand some day.

Limitations forever ended.

The key to being ascended.

PERFECTLY IMPERFECT

Those we love will not always behave exactly how we desire them to be.

They make mistakes.

At least as we care to perceive them.

Making us question if we really know them at all.

Are they worthy of our love?

Actions temporarily changing who we think they are.

Yet can our judgement have been so impaired?

If we perceive those we love to be a certain way, this is our expectation of who they are.

In our experience of knowing them.

How they seem to be to us.

If we want to keep the love.

If the love is really unconditional.

Look past the illusion of who this fellow human was or is to us.

Needing to accept them faults and all.

Accepting all people have many facets.

And forgive them for being less than perfect sometimes…

Everyone is entitled to have a bleurgh day occasionally!

TIME TO MEET THE DREAM STEALERS

They thought that they could rain on his parade.

Thinking he listened to the points they made.

How often they use words of anger, looking for a fight.

Attempting to move him away from what he knows is right.

Reminding him of supposed failures will never ever work.

As their vitriol continues, with slander and a smirk.

The dream stealers never achieve a thing.

Nothing to feel proud of makes their heart sing.

For dream stealers he has much compassion.

Wishing they could share for life his passion.

Determination gets anyone anywhere, remains true.

Take that first step now; your life path is up to you.

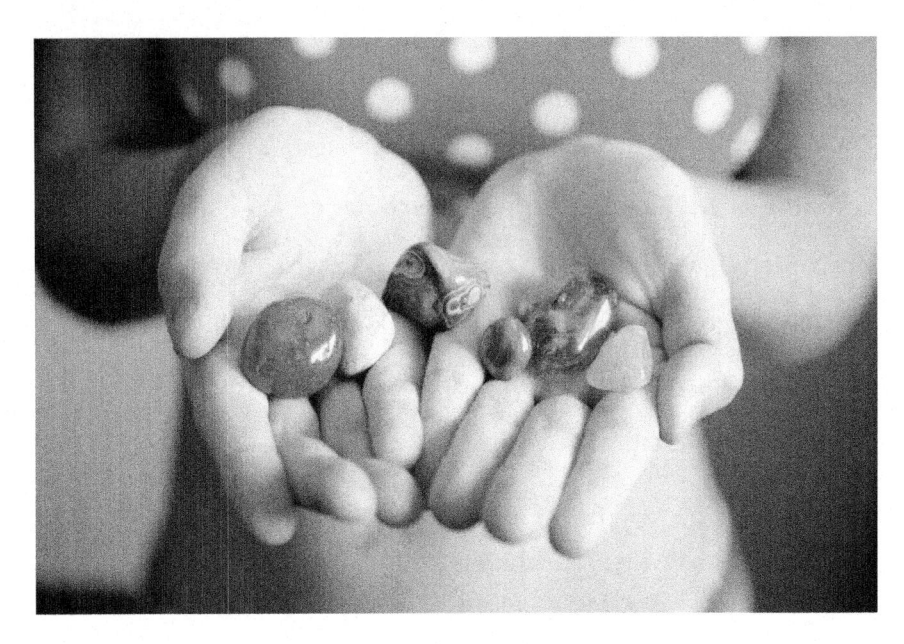

MAGIC GEMS

Rock Crystal of purest energy.

Smoky Quartz creating good chi.

Amethyst powerful healer.

Apache Tear karmic revealer.

Rose Quartz the love stone.

Carnelian "in the zone".

Tigereye Gold attracts wealth.

Malachite the aid to health.

Amazonite for lucky days.

Sunstone sunshine rays.

Bloodstone the blood tonic.

Snowflake Obsidian life harmonic.

Moonstone sweet dreams.

Black Obsidian reveals unseen.

Pink Agate have a good rest.

Flourite for passing a test.

Blue Obsidian wish making.

Green Jade for stomach aching.

Blue Howlite pure happiness.

Amber for financial success.

Orange Calcite much laughter.

Rainbow Moonstone happy ever after…

BEAUTY OF YOUR NATURE

Returning to innocence.

Your inner you of you.

Innocent as a small child.

Attuned to learn from nature.

The clearest sky.

The breeze cleansing.

Warm sun on your back.

Guided by the stars at night.

Infinity mirrored within.

Purest beauty.

The beauty of pure love.

WHO IS CREATING YOU?

Intellectual

Ineffectual

Tall

Small

Peasant

Pleasant

Older

Bolder

Reliable

Unreliable

Weird

Feared

Healing

Unfeeling

Visionary

Misery

Nationalist

Capitalist

Frightened

Enlightened

Our thoughts beating like drums.

Make sure they are always good ones.

Our choice to choose our words.

Their flight before us like birds.

Getting back what we give out.

A truth beyond any doubt.

The change you want is your choice.

Attention to your quiet inner voice.

Peace and Love purely given.

The past laid to rest, forgiven.

Anything feeling wrong to get rid of.

The core of life manifesting pure love.

DRAGONS

The still point.

Emanating inner calm.

Externalised.

Transcendent understanding.

Meditation.

Absolute power.

Satori – Dean Fraser

Never seen.

Yet tangible.

Impossible to know.

Yet all knowing.

Elusive.

Yet in everything.

Wisdom pervading.

Beyond logic.

Poise naturally.

Elegant actions.

Serenity deep within.

Attuned to source.

Spiritual warrior.

Advocate of peace.

The watercourse.

Running through us all.

Empowered action.

Dragon King.

THE LOVING ENDING

Living at peace with all that makes you…well, you!
This is home…simply takes a change in point of view.
Being happy in your skin, everywhere feels like home.
Constantly at home wherever you choose to roam…

I cannot claim personal credit for anything I create. And I do find myself continually amazed by the creative process and fascinated to see what next is produced through me! - Dean Fraser

Books And Audios By

Dean Fraser

A Healing For Gaia

Beyond Poetry

The Poems Less Spoken

The Spark Of Understanding

Walking Our Talk is Easy, Right?

Available from the Dean Fraser's official website

www.deanfrasercentral.com

WALKING OUR TALK IS EASY, RIGHT?

Short stories to awaken your inner mojo

Dean Fraser

Printed in Great Britain
by Amazon